# Christianity
# 101

*"And in Antioch the disciples were first called Christians."*

Bread of Life International Ministries

# Christianity 101
## Table of Contents

# Chapter 1
# Are You A Christian?

More than half of the people in the United States call themselves Christians because they go to church and are declared Catholics, Presbyterians, Lutherans, Methodists, Baptists, Four Square, Pentecostals, Charismatics... (the list goes on and on). But what does the Bible say a Christian is? "The disciples were called Christians first at Antioch," (this is from Acts 11:26, read all of it). Now, why would the disciples be called Christians? There were no churches (church buildings) there, indeed, they started the churches, and it wasn't based on them being of any denomination either. No, it was because of two things, whom they belonged to and who they imitated. The word **Christian** means little Christ, so they were called Christians because they went around town acting like (imitating) Christ or, a better way of saying that,

7

operating under, in and by the anointing and moved with compassion. A Christian is also one who belongs to Christ-God and His family.

In John 14:12 Jesus says, "I tell you for certain that if you have faith in me, you will do the same things that I am doing. You will do even greater things, now that I am going back to the Father." (Contemporary English Version) (By the way, that word "faith" means put your total trust in, have confidence in and rely upon).

So, you who claim faith in Jesus, do you do what He had done, do you do the greater works? Some would say, 'Yeah, I do all the healing stuff in His name, I cast out devils in His name. Yeah, I do what He did.' But Jesus said in Matt. 7:22-23,

"Many will say to me on that day, 'Lord, Lord, did we not prophesy in your name, and in your name drive out demons and perform many miracles?' Then I will tell them plainly, 'I never knew you. Away

8

from    me,    you    evildoers!'"    (New
International Version).


Well, why did Jesus call them evildoers, why did
He never know them?  They were Christians, weren't they?
Yes, they were Christians, or at least they were born again.
But now, let me give you this illustration and maybe you
can catch the message.  John and Carol had a son, he was a
son of John from birth.  JR. grew up being afraid of his dad
but did everything that he was supposed to do.  But because
he was afraid of his dad, a dad who really loved his son, JR.
took the orders from his mom or another brother or sister
and would only talk to them, not to his dad.  Because of
JR's attitude toward his dad, John never even knew his son,
whom he loved.   In this neighborhood where they lived
there were only two big families, sure there were more but
they all came from these two, they were the family of the
Goodson's (John's family) and the Badden's (the family of
John's enemy).  When John and his whole big family was
going to move to another state JR. came to John and said,
"John, I want to go with you.  I did everything that you
wanted me to do."  To this John replied, " Who are you?
You must be a Badden, get out of here."  Why didn't John
know his own son?  Called him a Badden, why?

A Frenchman was driving down the street one day,
aimlessly because he was lost.  Someone showed him the

right way to get where he wanted to go. After he arrived he needed some money for a new car, his broke down, but he could not talk to the banker because he didn't know the language and there was no one there to translate.

When you came to Christ (got born again into the family of God) you were led by someone, somehow. But now you want to communicate with your heavenly Father (we'll use the words **communicate** and **worship** as meaning this same thing here because you must communicate in order to worship). Jesus said in John 4:24, "God is spirit, and his worshipers must worship in spirit and in truth." Worshipping in spirit, the spirit of man is the heart of man, so those who worship in spirit must be worshipping with their whole heart. Worshipping in truth, truth is God's language; He spoke the Word of God so that is truth. So, to give a W.T. paraphrase of John 4:24 (under the authority of God), "God is the Spirit, so those who worship Him must worship Him from the heart and with the Word of God." Where it said "and" it meant and, "and" is an addition term meaning plus. So, what Jesus was and is saying is that you can't worship just with the heart but not with the Word, nor was/is He saying that your worship can be with the Word even if it's not from the heart. No!!! It must be both from the heart and with the Word.

# Being a Christian
# Excuse or Reason

Are you a Christian? Are you born again, truly a Christian? Ya know, some people, and I used to fit in this category, use the fact that they are Christians as an excuse for not being the best at what they do. They would do something foolish and then say, "Well, the Lord told me. . ." They would use Christianity as an excuse for ignorance. Then they would use a Bible verse to back themselves up, they would say, "After all, James said, 'Do you not know that friendship with the world is enmity with God? Whoever therefore wants to be a friend of the world makes himself an enemy of God,' (James 4:4)."

Well, that is part of what James 4:4 says but who was James talking to? The two verses before that plus the beginning of that verse tells whom James was talking to, it says,

> "You lust and do not have. You murder and covet and cannot obtain. You fight and war. Yet you do not have because you do not ask. You ask and do not receive, because you ask amiss, that you may spend it on your pleasures. Adulterers and

adulteresses!" (James 4:2-4a New King James Version).

But there are those, Christians, who go in the opposite direction where knowledge is concerned. They might say, "The Bible says, 'My people are destroyed for lack of knowledge,' (Hosea 4:6) so I should know what's going on in the world that I live in." Again, that's only a part of what that verse says, the whole verse will tell you what God is talking about,

"My people are destroyed for lack of knowledge. Because you have rejected knowledge, I also will reject you from being priest for Me; Because you have forgotten the law of your God, I also will forget your children." (Hosea 4:6 New King James Version).

So, you can see there that God wasn't talking to everyone but only those who He has set in position to teach others of the law. And the law then was the Law of Moses, but the law now is the Law of love. But anyway, these people that use this excuse think that by watching the news

12

constantly they will know and won't be destroyed, the only thing wrong with that is that the very thing that they think is knowledge is destroying them.

God wants to establish His covenant on the Earth, and He wants to use us, you and me, as Christians to do it. So, how are we going to do this? Well, I would think we would have to know His covenant to show His covenant to the world. Then we must speak His Words and do what He tells us to do and expect what He said to come to pass.

Now, if you are going to buy a car you should know a little bit about the car that you're going to buy, actually the more you know about the car the better. If you're going to get married, I'm not saying you need to shop around, you had better know as much as you can about the woman or man who you are going to marry, and I don't mean, "She's a fox." If God points her out to you as your future wife there's a real possibility that she will be your wife. But, even still, you better get to know her and let her get to know you, and I'm not talking about having sex. Find out what God says about the situation, the woman or man, or the car, or house, or whatever it is.

And if you are planning to go into business. . . Ya know, I, personally, failed in a few businesses not because I wasn't enthusiastic but because I didn't know what I was doing and because I relied to much on other people and also myself and not on God and what He had taught me.

13

There is an old adage that says, "If you fail to plan, you plan to fail." Well, whether you believe that or not why would you go into business selling and servicing computers locally if you didn't know anything about sales, people or computers or service or the competition? Make a business plan and have someone, a business executive, check it out.

When you do something because you say, "God told me to do that," you had better expect God to take care of your situation and don't be wishy-washy. And if you are going to rely on God in one area you had better be prepared to rely on Him in all areas. But that doesn't mean you don't have to know what you're doing. Don't play dumb and expect God to rescue you.

# Chapter 2
# Christianity is an Action

> "And though I have *the gift of*
> prophecy, and understand all mysteries and
> all knowledge, and though I have all faith,
> so that I could remove mountains, but have
> not love, I am nothing." (1 Corinthians 13:2
> New King James Version).

Let's look at that verse a minute. It says, ". . .the
GIFT of prophecy," Now, how can one get a gift of the
Holy Spirit (1 Corinthians 12:10) unless he is first born
again (born of God, born of love) and baptized in the Holy
Spirit (God)? So, Paul, the writer of Corinthians, is saying
he has love because he has the gift of prophecy, but then he
says, 'but if I use this gift (which only comes from love)
without love I am nothing." It makes no sense when you

really look at that verse without taking some things into
consideration.

> "And this is his commandment, That
> we should believe on the name of his Son
> Jesus Christ, and love one another, as he
> gave us commandment." (1 John 3:23 New
> King James Version).

How did Jesus give us commandment to love?
Well, to answer that we would have to see what Jesus did;
so look in the gospels.

> "Most assuredly, I say to you, he
> who believes in Me, the works that I do he
> will do also; and greater *works* than these he
> will do, because I go to My Father." (John
> 14:12 New King James Version).

When you read the four gospels you see that Jesus
went around doing good and healing all, He cast out
demons when it was needed, He corrected wrong thoughts
and words (**with tact**), He used his faith to the limit for us

as He knew that God was taking care of Him, and He didn't fear nor worry.

The verse, 1 Corinthians 13:2, also says that Paul had faith to remove mountains. Now that kind of faith works by love, so Paul must have had love too have that kind of faith. But why did he say, ". . .but have not love,"? Look at this verse,

> "For as the body without the spirit is dead, so faith without works is dead also." (James 2:26 New King James Version).

What would be the works of your faith? Corresponding action. If your faith was for buying something what would the corresponding action (the works) be? Would they be giving to the poor? That's an admirable thing to do but no. I would suppose the corresponding actions would be getting the money, doing price checking to find the best deal and then you pay for it.

So, we're seeing, here, that what Paul was saying is that if he had love but did not *act* upon love it was the same as not having love in the first place.

I'm sure you all know or have heard these verses quoted, "The just shall live by faith," "And walk in love," well these are telling us that the Christian life is an action life. An easier way to say that is just to say Christianity is an action word.

I want to quote to you something that Jesus said in Matthew 7:21,

> "Not everyone who says to Me, 'Lord, Lord,' shall enter the kingdom of heaven, but he who does the will of My Father in heaven. Many will say to Me in that day, 'Lord, Lord, have we not prophesied in Your name, cast out demons in Your name, and done many wonders in Your name?' And then I will declare to them, 'I never knew you; depart from Me, you who practice lawlessness!'" (New King James Version).

They were prophesying, they casting out demons, they were doing wonders in the name of love (Jesus). But why did Jesus cast them away and tell them to depart? Well, there are two reasons; 1) being that they didn't have intimacy with Him and 2) because of what Paul said in 1 Corinthians 13:2, they did not have (operate in) love. Jesus wasn't denying the fact that they had a 'born again experience' and they where, indeed, born of love. No, what

18

He was stating, and is stating today, is that if you are born of love you should let love be shown in you, let love be your guide rather than doing these things to show that you are a Christian. That does not mean that you shouldn't do those things, but let love guide you. What they where doing was bragging, saying, 'Look at me, this is what I did.'

So, Jesus is not looking for a Christian couch potato and He is not looking for a Christian braggart and neither is He looking for a Christian workaholic. What I see that He is looking for is someone whom He can lead, guide and operate through. Allow me to paraphrase 1 Corinthians 13:2, "If I have all the gifts of the Spirit and can understand all mysteries and have all knowledge, and if I have all faith to move mountains, but don't let love guide me, use me, work through me, I am nothing but a man destined for failure."

Now, let me show you some of the things that should characterize a person who is operating in love, to do that I will show you 1 Corinthians 13:4-7 from the Amplified Bible:

"Love endures long *and* is patient and kind; love never is envious *nor* boils over with jealousy, is not boastful *or* vainglorious (holding on to self-pride), does not display itself haughtily. It is not conceited (arrogant and inflated with pride); it is not rude (unmannerly) *and* does not act unbecomingly. Love (God's love in us) does not insist on it's own rights *or* it's own way, *for* it is not self-seeking; it is not touchy *or* fretful (fearful) *or* resentful (it does not hold a grudge); it takes no account of evil done to it [it pay no attention to a suffered wrong]. It does not rejoice at injustice *and* unrighteousness, but rejoices when right *and* truth prevail. Love bears up under anything *and* everything that comes (it never fails in love), is ever ready to believe the best of every person, it's hopes are fadeless under all circumstances, and it endures everything without weakening] (it can stand)."

We all need work in this area. Are you willing to grow and learn love from love?

# Fig Tree Christians

> "So he said to the vinedresser, See here! For these three years I have come looking for fruit on this fig tree and I find none. Cut it down! Why should it continue also to use up the ground [to deplete the soil, intercept the sun, and take up room]?" (Luke 13:7 Amplified Bible).

Jesus compared believers to fig trees. He said that this farmer came every year for three years and found no fruit. That tells me that a fig tree should have fruit the first year because the farmer came looking for fruit every year. A Christian is supposed to show fruit in the first year of growth.

I accepted Jesus as Lord when I was in high school. But I didn't start growing until I received the baptism in the Holy Spirit, four years later. Although I had the fruit of the Spirit in me, I wasn't growing in Him. If, after I had received the Holy Spirit I still wasn't producing any fruit I would have been in trouble.

I just saw something and caught the irony of it. The farmer came three years and found no fruit; I was born again for three years yet wasn't showing fruit. He told his servant to cut it down; but the servant gave an ultimatum, he said that he will work on it and that in another year, the fourth year, if there was no fruit then he would cut it down; I was baptized in the Holy Spirit and began to show fruit in the fourth year. Can you see the similarities?

Now, what fruit is Jesus talking about, the fruit of your lips (your words), the fruit of prayer (answered prayer), reproduction fruit (reproducing after your kind), or the fruit of the Spirit (the attributes of Jesus)? Well, since this parable is about a fig tree and it's fruit you would think it would be reproduction fruit. I submit to you that it could very well be the fruit of your lips (your words lining up with the godly expressions). You may think it's some other fruit, don't throw rocks.

"But he replied to him, Leave it alone, sir, [just] this one more year, till I dig around it and put manure [on the soil]," (Luke 13:8 Amplified Bible).

**Manure** is fertilizer, to help the tree grow. The Holy Spirit is here by His baptism to help us grow; I mean no disrespect, but in this parable the manure would be the sweet savory Holy Spirit baptism, He helps us grow.

"And seeing in the distance a fig tree in leaf, he went to see if he could find anything on it. When he came to it, he found nothing but leaves, for it was not the season for figs," (Mark 11-13 Amplified Bible). Let's take out that "for it was not the season for figs."

In this visual, physical comparison of a fig tree to believers the tree had been there for, probably, many years. When Jesus saw it, the fig tree wanted to appear full and plush; if it were a believer it would be saying, "Hey, look at me, Jesus, I'm a Christian." But when Jesus went over to it to get some fruit off it He found nothing. Now, that sounds a little like the way I find many 'church goers' outside of the four walls of the church. Inside, they make a show of being a Christian, *maybe*, but when I see them outside they seem to blend in with the rest of the world; they talk the same, they react the same, they even look the same (weight wise). Do any of those people bring anyone to Christ, outside of the church building?

That's why Jesus cured the fig tree. Where was the fruit? It may show inside the church, *maybe*, but that's not where the Christian is to be fruitful, think about it. The measure of a Christian is not taken inside the church building *or with your Christian friends*; the measure of a

23

Christian is taken outside, at home, among those who don't know or like Jesus or you. So, where is your fruit?

If you had received Jesus as Lord and yet you are not growing or showing fruit, no worries; just start now. The rapture of the church has not come yet—I don't know when it will come, but it will be soon, that I know—and that is the last time that your fruit will be checked for, before the end. If you don't have fruit then you will suffer the curse, if you show fruit you may be spared. After the rapture you have seven years to work on it; but those seven years will be the hardest years you could ever dream to go through if you want to be a Christian.

# Chapter 3
# Christianity

I want you to think for a minute about what it means *to you* to be a Christian. What does Christianity mean? According to the English dictionary it is a religion. Some of you will probably think of Christianity as a belief system, believing that once you have confessed Jesus as your savior then you are set for life and you will go to heaven. Some others think of Christianity as a life style of spreading the word about Jesus.

"To this He answered, "No worries. That time is not now, and you don't need to know when it will be. Just know this, you shall be enveloped in power once you are baptized in the Holy Spirit. This must be by your acceptance because the Father will

25

never force anything upon anyone. But when you have this power you will witness—represent and spread the good news—of me, starting at home then spreading out," (Acts 1:7-8 Steadfast in Honor).

In Acts 1:1 we see that Jesus started a work in the Earth. If He started the work and He is alive still then it's pretty obvious that He wants to continue that work until it is done and we all go home.

So, while Christianity is a life style of spreading the word, it is more than that. Here is what Jesus said,

"Very truly I tell you, whoever believes in me will do the works I have been doing, and they will do even greater things than these, because I am going to the Father. And I will do whatever you ask in my name, so that the Father may be glorified in the Son. (John 14:12-13 New International Version).

So, if you truly believe that Jesus is Lord then you will act like He is Lord and you will do what He did; if you don't do what He did then maybe you don't truly believe what you say you believe. Hey, don't get mad at the messenger if you don't like the message. Some will say that that verse correctly says that if someone believes then they can do what He did. Ok, so if there is a need and you can do what Jesus did then why don't you? Others might think that just because they are pastors or whatever they don't have to anymore (as if they use to before they were put in those positions). No one is exempt from verse 12. I'm stepping on toes I know, but God will heal your toes if you will let Him by growing with this article.

You will notice that Jesus said, "And I will do whatever you ask in my name…" The "And" there could just as easily be "And *then*," meaning if you don't he won't. The other "and" could be a plain and or it could also be and then, meaning you've got to be doing the first part before you can do the second part, and when you get to doing the second part you should still be doing the first part.

So, Christianity is more than just a belief system, more than just spreading the word that Jesus is who he is (savior and to some, Lord). While Christianity is both of those, it is also a set of actions. Jesus also said this about how we can recognize true believers,

"Whoever believes and is baptized
**(As I am, in the Holy Spirit of my Father)**
will be saved, but whoever does not believe
**(Like me)** will be condemned. And these
signs will accompany those who believe
**(This is how believers will be recognized)**:
In my name they will drive out demons
**(Where there is one)**; they will speak in
new tongues; they will pick up snakes with
their hands **(When necessary)**; and when
they drink deadly poison **(When tricked)**, it
will not hurt them at all; they will place their
hands on sick people **(When needed)**, and
they *will* get well," (Mark 16:16-18 New
International Version)**(Boldface added for
clarity)**.


You are right, I'm not the one who is supposed to
judge whether you are a Christian or not; you are. But I
think Jesus was pretty clear about what a believer would
do. So, you judge yourself: Are you a true believing
Christian or are you a pretender? I won't tell anyone, but
the devil will because he/it is the accuser of all, not just the
brethren.

If you gave it good, considerable thought and have found that you are a pretender, you can still make it right. Just pray this prayer out loud and in your heart.

*1. "Father, I accept Jesus as my Lord.*

*2. I repent of not doing this before, that's sin.*

*3. I am determined to believe that you raised Jesus from the dead.*

*4. I commit my life to you and to doing your will.*

*5. Jesus, baptize and anoint me in the Holy Spirit."*

Now open your mouth and give control over your tongue too the Holy Spirit. You won't understand what you're saying but, no worries, you don't need to. It's a secret code that—I believe—neither the devil nor man knows.

# Chapter 4
## Are You A Christian Or Not?

When a man and a woman get married, the Bible says, they are one flesh.

> "Therefore shall a man leave his father and his mother, and shall cleave unto his wife: and they shall be one flesh." (Genesis 2:24 King James Version) (read the verses around it).

In truth they are joined in spirit also, if they are not they had better make the effort to be or they shouldn't be married.

The physical is meant to be an example of the spiritual, if it's not it's out of order. So, when a man or woman becomes born again he marries Jesus and becomes one spirit with his Spirit. So, a man marries Jesus, gets born again, his spirit becomes one with Jesus' Spirit. A man and his wife might have a to-do and quit on their marriage, this is not God's way but man's, God's way is mercy. A divorce does hurt very much on both sides, although they may think they are better off they do hurt and they're never the same. If a man commits apostasy against Jesus it will kill him.

"The acts of the sinful nature are obvious: sexual immorality, impurity and debauchery; idolatry and witchcraft; hatred, discord, jealousy, fits of rage, selfish ambition, dissensions, factions and envy; drunkenness, orgies, and the like. I warn you, as I did before, that those who live like this will not inherit the kingdom of God.

"But the fruit of the Spirit is love, joy, peace, patience, kindness, goodness, faithfulness, gentleness and self-control. Against such things there is no law. Those who belong to Christ Jesus have crucified the sinful nature with its passions and

desires. Since we live by the Spirit, let us
keep in step with the Spirit. Let us not
become conceited, provoking and envying
each other." (Galatians 5:19-26 New
International Version).

That's not talking about being baptized in the Holy
Spirit, it's talking about living for Jesus and letting Jesus
live through you. See, Jesus is the fruit, offspring, of the
Holy Spirit and so these nine traits (love, joy, peace,
patience, kindness, goodness, faithfulness, gentleness and
self-control) are all characteristics of Jesus, who is Love.
But just because you are born again I can't expect you to be
fluent in all of these characteristics, you need the Holy
Spirit to lead, guide and teach you how.

I, really, don't care who you are; you can be the
greatest in the kingdom of God (so it would seem), living
love to the best of your ability. And you might even seem
to be oozing joy, peace, patience, kindness, goodness,
faithfulness, gentleness and self-control as much as you
think possible. You might be on the streets all the time,
when you're not working, witnessing to Jesus, winning folk
over to Christ by the truckload. You give and give until
you can't give any more. But are you sure you are living to
the fullest extent of what God wants you to live, what does
the Bible say about it?

Jesus didn't tell us everything that we need to know in the three and a half years of His ministry, "I have yet many things to say unto you, but ye cannot bear them now." (John 16:12 King James Version) But Paul wrote much more of what He had to say in the epistles. Jesus said that the Holy Spirit would be our teacher and Paul told us that the Holy Spirit would help us in prayer also.

When Jesus was born He did not *automatically* have the Holy Spirit, He had to accept Him. Jesus is to be an example of how we are to live (not times and customs but having the victory and not cowering down or compromising), if Jesus had to accept the Holy Spirit then so do we.

# Be A Christian

How did you become an American? Most of you were born American, I'm sure. But, for American's at least, there is one more way that you can achieve citizenship. Live in America for seven years, at least, and then apply for citizenship. Upon application approval you go to a place and recite an oath of loyalty to America and are given citizenship. It's something like that. But the thing is, you are now an American not an African or any other nationality, you may want to hold onto your roots but your not that nationality anymore.

Okay, you were once a citizen of the kingdom of darkness (being a sinner, one who practices sin) and satan, the devil, was your king. Then someone told you about the kingdom of God and you wanted to become a citizen of this beautiful kingdom. But, to become a citizen of this kingdom you can't simply apply, recite some pledge (whether you mean it not), and it be given, you have to be born into it. Now, before you get that stupid notion that I am kicking you out, let me tell you that none of us were born into this kingdom strait from our mother's womb, if you think you were think again (and don't get cute on me).

Sure we must be born into this kingdom, born again. Jesus, the Lord of this wonderful kingdom, said that you have to be born again to, even, see the kingdom. That meant you must change your focus and start looking and believe in the kingdom. He is saying that you can't even see the kingdom unless/until you believe in Him.

John 3:3, "Jesus answered and said to him, 'Most assuredly, I say to you, unless one is born again, he cannot see the kingdom of God.'" (New King James Version).

But the Word of God, the handbook of the kingdom, doesn't leave it at that. It tells us that if we believe strong enough then we will confess what we believe.

Luke 6:45, "A good man out of the good treasure of his heart brings forth good; and an evil man out of the evil treasure of his heart brings forth evil. For out of the abundance of the heart his mouth speaks." (New King James Version) (Read the rest of that chapter).

So, there are similarities between becoming an American and becoming a Christian, one in the kingdom of God—the family of God, body of Christ. Just because you applied to become an American citizen doesn't mean you will be, they could turn you down. But if you ask to become a Christian God will never turn you down, and no man, woman or child has that right no matter what you did in the past. Look at Paul, he was radically persecuting the Church to the point of killing Christians, but even he was not turned down. To become a Christian you must believe in Jesus, the Lord, and confess what you believe, your oath of loyalty, your pledge of allegiance to the kingdom, to Jesus, just like to become an American you have to make the oath of loyalty, that pledge of allegiance to America.

And, in both cases you are not a citizen of the former kingdom anymore, you can't hold two citizenships, either you are African, Asian, European, Australian or an American. Either you are a citizen of the kingdom of darkness (being a sinner, one who practices sin), and satan is you Lord and Master, or you are a citizen of the kingdom of God (kingdom of light) (this done by the new birth, being born again) and Jesus is your Lord. There is no straddling the fence with either one; it's either one or the other and never both.

When you become/became an American you got to enjoy all the rights and freedoms of being an American. But there are responsibilities to being an American also, you are not supposed to call yourself an African or Asian or Australian, which some do. And you are required to obey the laws of America. Likewise when you become/became a Christian, (*not* a sinner anymore).

"Therefore, if anyone *is* in Christ, *he* *is* a new creation; old things have passed away; behold, all things have become new." (2 Corinthians 5:17 New King James Version) (The old things that past away

were the sinful nature, the old sinner nature,
and the selfish nature).

You now have the ability to enjoy all the rights and
freedoms of being a Christian, but you also have
responsibilities, you have no right to be calling yourself an
old sinner and you should be finding out what Jesus said
and wants you to do.

When you are an American you have made a pledge
to America, you belong to America. And when you are a
Christian you have made a pledge and you belong to Christ.
From Acts 11:26 "And the disciples were first called
Christians in Antioch." One definition of Christian is little
Christs, these men were going all around acting like they
were Jesus Himself, not just within their church group or
behind the walls of the church house. But how could they
do that unless they belonged to Christ? They could not
have. Remember the seven sons of Sceva! They tried to
act like Christians but the devil knew they weren't.

So, now my charge to you. If you are a Christian
BE A CHRISTIAN!

www.ingramcontent.com/pod-product-compliance
Lightning Source LLC
Chambersburg PA
CBHW060643030426
42337CB00018B/3422